RAISING AND MENTORING YOUR CHILDREN TO SUCCESS

How We Raised Five Children Who Are Now Called Dr. Stoddard

Dr. Mary A. Whitlock Stoddard

BK Royston Publishing
Jeffersonville, IN 47131
http://www.bkroystonpublishing.com
bkroystonpublishing@gmail.com

© Copyright – 2025

All Rights Reserved. No part of this book may be reproduced, stored in a retrieval system, or transmitted by any means without the written permission of the author.

Cover Photo: benstevens@benjaminstevensphotography.com
Cover Design: Elite Book Covers

ISBN-13: 978-1-967282-82-1

Printed in the United States of America

Dedication

To my Lord and Savior Jesus Christ, who is my guiding light.

To the late L & Leola Rebecca Allen Whitlock for defining loyalty, persistence, and commitment. To my siblings for always being supportive. To my children: Shana, Damian, Carmella, Erica, and Serena, you are all great in your own individuality and my joy. To my husband, together we can do great things. To Professor Serena Williams and Judge Donald Johnson, many people could do many things if they had friends like you. To all my mentees and church family members who understand that those who achieve success are truly a product of the village. Words cannot express the importance of each of your support and dedication to the many accomplishments we have achieved as a family. We do not take it for granted that your very presence in our lives has been a great impact and for that we are forever grateful.

ABOUT THE AUTHOR

Dr. Mary A Whitlock Stoddard, B.S., M.S., M.B.A., J.D., Ed.D., R.D.L.D., Esq., completed a Bachelor of Science in food and Nutrition from Southern University, Baton Rouge, Louisiana. A Masters of Arts in Management and a Masters of Business Administration from Webster University, St. Louis, Missouri. A Juris Doctor at the Salmon P. Chase College of Law, Northern Kentucky University, Highland Heights, Kentucky. A Doctorate in Education at Spalding University, Louisville, Kentucky.

Stoddard holds two licenses, one as a Registered Dietitian and the other as an admitted attorney to the practice law, Kentucky State Bar Association. At the writing of this book, Dr. Mary Stoddard (aka Dr. Stoddard #2) has been married over 45 years to Dr. Marcus Stoddard, M.D. (aka Dr. Stoddard #1), and is the mother of five children.

Dr. Marcus Stoddard, FACC, FAHA, FASE

Marcus F. Stoddard, M.D., FACC, FAHA, FASE, is also a professor of Medicine, Director, Non-Invasive Cardiology, Director of Echocardiography Lab, UofL Health - UofL Hospital, Medical Director, Cardiovascular Imaging, UofL Health. ,Dr. Stoddard holds a Doctor of Medicine from The Johns Hopkins University College of Medicine, and a Bachelor of Arts from Holy Cross College. He completed his internship and residency in Internal Medicine at Saint Louis University Medical Center and also his fellowship in Cardiovascular medicine.

While at the University of Louisville Dr. Stoddard also received additional training in Nuclear Cardiology. His clinical *expertise* is in General Cardiology; Echocardiography; Echocardiographically Guided Resynchronization; Trans Esophageal echocardiography, Cardiac CT; Nuclear Cardiology.

Dr. Stoddard is highly regarded for his teaching skills in training new cardiologists, patient care, and research.

Dr. Shana Stoddard, Ph.D.

Shana, otherwise known as Dr Stoddard #3. She holds a Ph.D. from the University of Mississippi in Chemistry and Biochemistry. After earning her PhD, Dr. Stoddard continued her studies at St. Jude Children's Research Hospital as a Postdoctoral Research Associate in the Department of Radiological Sciences. She joined the faculty at Rhodes College in 2015 as a William Randolph Hearst Teaching Fellow and joined the Department of Chemistry as an assistant professor in 2017.

Shana is now a tenured professor at Rhodes College. Shana Holds an M.Ed. Freed-Hardeman University Curriculum and Instruction: emphasis Special Education; Bachelor of Science from Prairie View A&M University in Chemistry and is a tenured professor of biochemistry at Rhodes College. Dr. Stoddard's "Molecular Immunotherapeutic Research" (MIR) lab research program focuses on improving patient outcomes with autoimmune disorders, in particular primary membranous nephritis (PMN), through the development of auto-antibody-specific inhibitors, antigen-specific therapies, as well as novel methods for the development of antigen-specific therapies.

Dr. Shana Stoddard was awarded the 2023 Silvia Ronco Innovative Mentor Award. The award was established to recognize an investigator working with undergraduates who has had significant impact in the careers of the students. Dr. Stoddard is a 2023 CSN Scholar-in-Residence. Shana is also the 2021 recipient of the Mentor Award presented by the Council on Undergraduate Research's (CUR) Health Sciences Division. Shana received the American Chemical Society Trailblazer Award for Chemist in September 2025.

Dr. Damian L. Stoddard, Ph.D.

Damian, aka Dr. Stoddard # 5, is a professor in Engineering Science at the University of Mississippi. Dr. Stoddard holds a Ph.D. in Mechanical Engineering from the University of Mississippi, and a M.E. in Engineering Science, also from the University of Mississippi. Dr. Stoddard obtained his Bachelor of Science in Mechanical Engineering, from Prairie View A&M University.

Damian is a *tenure track professor* at the University of Mississippi. Assistant Professor, Mechanical Engineering and Assistant Professor, General Engineering.

Damian holds an interest in the area of Composite structures and mechanics, Impact and crashworthiness, Dynamic characterization, Metallic foams, Additive manufacturing, Armor design. Damian is the principal investigator for the subcontractor award for the UNLV Broad Agency announcement which is a 4.8 million dollar grant to study Rapid Processing of Ultra-Light Weight Materials in Infrastructure Applications.

Damian is married to Dr. Okoia Uket Stoddard, PharmD/Ph.D. in Pharmacology, and father of twin sons Levi and Gabriel.

Dr. Carmella Stoddard, Ph.D.

Carmella, aka Dr. Stoddard #7, holds a Ph.D in Sociology from the Department of Sociology 2024, at the University of California Los Angeles (UCLA). Carmella's interests include social networks, computational methods, culture, social psychology, and sociological theory. Her dissertation examines romantic, sexual, and affiliative relationship networks of National Longitudinal Study of Adolescent to Adult Health (Add Health) respondents and celebrity entertainers. Using multiple datasets, she computationally assesses how multiplexity, status homophily, and negative proscriptions shape underlying network structure. In doing so, she contributes to network analysis and sociological theory by testing the scope conditions of complex relational configurations. Broadly speaking, her interest in dynamic network analysis, intergroup relations, and offers convincing evidence that celebrity networks constitute respectable datasets.

Carmella's interest is dynamic network analytics and intergroup relations. Carmella holds a B.A. in American Studies and Ethnicity from the University of Southern California and an M.A. in Communication from the University of Massachusetts Amherst Carmella focus is in Substantive Topics: Sociology of Celebrity, Intergroup Relations, Relationship Formation, Media Representation Subfield: Computational Sociology, Social Networks, Social Theory, Critical Theory, Culture, Social Psychology, Race & Ethnicity, Quantitative Methods Carmella's research interests also include network analysis, norms, romantic and sexual relationship networks, and group dynamics.

Dr. Erica Stoddard, M.D.

Erica, aka Dr. Stoddard # 4, completed her interventional Endovascular Surgical Neuroradiology fellowship and Vascular Neurology Fellowship at the University of Minnesota in 2025. Dr. Stoddard completed her internship and residency at the Sky Ridge Medical Center in Denver, Colorado. She completed her medical school studies at the University of Cincinnati College of Medicine after earning her undergraduate degree at Rice University in Houston, Texas.

Erica has been accepted into the Device Fellowship at the Institute of Engineering in Medicine at the University of Minnesota.

Dr. Serena Stoddard, DVM

Serena is our youngest known as, Dr. Stoddard #6. She holds a Doctor of Veterinary Medicine from Tuskegee University. Serena completed her undergraduate studies at the University of Missouri, obtaining a Bachelor of Science in Animal Science. Serena has currently completed a Small Animal Medicine & Surgery Internship at the University of Georgia Veterinary Teaching Hospital.

At the time of this writing, Serena is completing an internship in Avian, Exotic and Zoological Medicine at Colorado State University. After which she will enter the Master of Science Program with a focus on Assisted Reproductive Technologies specializations. In this program, she will focus on human and animal embryology. She will undergo in-depth lab training in oocyte collection, in vitro fertilization, cryopreservation, and other related procedures. After which, she will seek a residency or fellowship in zoological medicine.

Serena's long-term goal is to become a board-certified theriogenologist and zoological medicine veterinarian.

Table of Contents

Dedication	iii
About the Author	iv
Profiles of all of the Dr. Stoddards	v
Introduction	xix
Background of the Family	1
The Road To Success - Expectations	9
The Road to Success is by Determination	19
Goals	25
Parental Observation to Identify Each Child's Capability, Identification of Characteristics, Traits and Passions	39
Parenting	59
Emotions, Environmental Factors, and Effects	83
Preparation for College	93
Religion	103
Summary of Tools For Success	111
Summary Of Take-A-Ways	119

Introduction

How do you do all that? How did you find the time? Too often, I have been asked these two questions. After I responded, the person would say to me "You should write a book, so others would know how they can do it as well." To fulfill that request and hopefully to assist others who live in the land of what I call the "I wish, I could, or I should have done that," this book is written with you in mind. It is my hope that it will encourage you to: pursue your life dreams, pass a legacy on to your children, and develop and execute goals. Regardless of your age, sex, economic status, environmental factors, the economy, your family makeup and or any other circumstances, my desire is that this book will be a catalyst for you to be all you have the potential to become.

Through these pages, I will discuss how to pass on to the next generations your values and keys to their success. A roadmap will be laid out detailing the characteristics and traits that promote success in their endeavors, even if they fail at a task. I will share experiences that represent the methods I used to raise my children and promote their ability to succeed.

The question; How did you do that? refers to the accomplishments I have achieved over the years, including having raised five children. I have obtained five degrees and two licensures. Each of our children have obtained terminal or professional degrees in a specific discipline resulting in them bearing the name of Doctor Stoddard. My true answer to the question above is by the grace of God, much prayer, dedication, sacrifice, and hard work. My children accomplish what many believe to be unusual or inconceivable—to have five children who are all accomplished successful professionals.

With the two questions in mind above, along with my mindset of unselfishness, I wanted to share the journey. At this point, you are probably wondering what makes me so special and why should you care about what I have accomplished. Honestly, there's nothing special about me, although many would disagree. I consider myself an everyday, ordinary person of great faith, with a lot of will power, determination, persistence, dedication, energy, loyalty, open-minded, driven, frailty, successfulness, passion, and most importantly I am a Christian. These are some of the same traits you possess along with an inkling of a want for more. Most parents desire their child to become all they have the capabilities of becoming. It is that inkling and belief that brought me to this point of success for me and our children.

Over the years, I have come to discover that I am a catalyst for helping others achieve their potential. I have also learned that as I boosted my husband and children in their successful endeavors, I gained a deeper understanding about myself, and learned to come to terms with the different positions I would need to fulfill and maintain, in order for them to be successful.

I hope the path I have traveled will inspire, guide, and assist you, your spouse, and or your child to excel and maximize their potential. In my previous book *110 Thought Provoking Quotes by Mary*, you will find these words "Acknowledging history by not repeating it yields wisdom as we make wise decisions." This quote means that the path I have already traveled to help my children succeed is history for me. However, it can be the source of wisdom to assist you in making wise decisions for you and your child. My path can be a guiding light to you and or your child's success.

My prayer for you is that God's blessings are with you and your child as you proceed toward your goals.

Background Of The Family

To understand the significance of the accomplishments of the Stoddard family, it is vital that you know our background. I was raised the daughter of a sharecropper father and a mother who worked in the school food service. We lived on a sharecropper's farm in Louisiana. I am the seventh child born out of sixteen children; however, only fourteen of us were raised together. We never had much in the way of material things, but we had both parents physically present. They gave us an introduction to four important things that would help us make our way off the farm and become prosperous: A belief in God, an understanding that siblings are an endless value in life, hard work, and hope for more in life. These four things were an introduction to God.

Our routine was to rise early with the sun to take care of farm animals, and then off to school during the school year. After school, we may have to go to the field. Although there were some days, we would have to miss school to pick cotton in the fields. Also, all the animals had to be attended to and secured for the night. During the summer months, the same routine but instead of going to school, we were off to the fields to chop cotton which is hoeing to remove the weeds from the cotton and soybeans. Additionally, we were responsible for hoeing the gardens and harvesting the garden produce as well. After the sun went down, we would come out from the fields and complete our chores. Those of us who had checked out books from the bookmobile would read those books. The bookmobile would run every two weeks and so we would get enough books to cover those two weeks until it is returned.

Our house was a small three bedroom and later expanded to four, then five bedrooms. It was a home where mom worked hard to keep clean and dry since the roof leaked in several places. There were holes in places where they were not supposed to be. There was no central air, but you could open the windows and invite the misquotes in as well. There was no central heat, and so wood had to be cut and split to keep the house heated by a wood heater in the winter.

As a sharecropper, my father did not own the land; instead, he worked the land and had to give a part of each crop as rent. I never knew if my father ever made any money on the farm, we picked pecans and sold them to add to our resources. This financial status was below poverty level. No one had a bed for themself it was an open bedroom for at least three or however many of the same sex existed at that time. There were one or two twin mattresses to share. We had a wood stove and eventually became high society and graduated to a gas stove.

We had limited resources, but we had great provision from God. There were plenty of natural fruits trees and pecan trees, which proved to be a valuable resource. Fruits such as grapes, muscadine, pears, peaches, plums, persimmons, blackberries, and fig trees. These fruits grew plentifully year after year. We grew most of our food in a large garden that consisted of tomatoes, corn, red potatoes, sweet potatoes, okra, squash, cucumber, green beans, green peas, purple hull peas, lima beans, carrots, greens mustard, cabbage, kale, turnip, and snap beans.

We milked the cows by hand one to two times a day. We drank it, made butter, buttermilk, heavy cream, and ice cream. We had chicken that provided eggs and meat. Additionally, we had pigs and cows, which provided us with meat.

There was a pond of water beside our house, and it provided fish. We never stock that pond, but it always provides catfish, bass, trout, bluegill, and other fish. I later learned that when there was heavy rain, and the water would cross the road, we could catch large trout fish because they would get caught in the wire fence. We had crawfish, which we would play with and then cook. The crawfish would make holes that they would dig anywhere on the farm, mostly around the pond, and we could use a string to draw them out of their hole since they would grab hold of anything in their reach.

We had an outhouse for the bathroom. This was a large hole dug in the ground and a wooden structure was built around it to give you some privacy, with or without a door. Nevertheless, this was the toilet. There was no money for toilet paper so any magazines that showed up in the mail became more than useful. Nothing was ever wasted. For example, because of the holes in the tin roof, rainwater would drip inside the house. Consequently, we placed pots around the room to collect the water for later use. Rainwater was great for washing clothes. We used a scrub board placed in a washtub. We also used the same tub to bathe in. The clothes were then hung on the clothesline outside to dry. We would have to keep an eye on the weather to make sure we brought the clothes in off the clothesline before it rained.

For a bath, we would heat water on the wood stove and transfer it to the washtub. For a long time, we used rainwater as a source of water. Later, we had a well and we could obtain water more consistently, albeit a little rusty but it was running water. We later added salt to remove some of the minerals from the water.

As a youth, I remember raising a large garden to feed the family, the hogs, cows, chickens, and working the fields, picking cotton, and hoeing the fields without receiving any pay. I remember missing school days to pick cotton, and if any of us missed the school bus, then our reward was to go to the fields to pick cotton.

We worked every day except Sunday; it was church day. Growing up, it was not an option to decide whether you were going to church; you better be there. When it was time to go to church, we would pile into the back of the pickup truck, and if you missed the truck, you had better start walking and get there before Sunday school ended. We would have Sunday school on Sunday mornings and church services on every third Sunday of the month. There was a prayer meeting on Wednesday nights. On Sundays after church, we would play basketball. We could sing in the choir, take our turn to teach Sunday school, and clean the church was a part of our responsibility. Church was and is the most important glue that held the family together. It is the glue that still holds our family together today.

Many prayers have been spoken that resulted in the great accomplishments the Stoddards have achieved in receiving our doctorates. We found, and hope you discover that the village is still very much needed to achieve success. Regarding my accomplishment, I hope you understand that the source of my strength is Jesus Christ and what He has made available to me as a resource. The saying "someone was praying for you" is true, as I pray regularly for the success of all the Dr. Stoddards.

My husband, Dr. Stoddard #1, was raised in the projects in Washington D.C. He is from a loving but dysfunctional family. His father was mostly absent from his life as his mother and father separated when he was young. His mother had other male supporters who encouraged him to be the best he could be. This led him to connect with Mike, who is still my husband's best friend. Marcus and Mike attended DeMatha High School and then went to Holy Cross College. They are and remain each other's support system to this day. This support between the two of them led them to become successful doctors also. Every success has some form of support system.

The Road To Success - Expectations

Our success in raising five children and helping each of them to become doctors in their own discipline was based on instilling in them that we have expectations of them, helping them develop goals, parental observation of each child's capability, identifying characteristics relevant to any particular discipline, individualistic traits, passions, faith, and prayer.

We had expectations for our children that they would be able to care for themselves. As parents it was our responsibility to ensure that our offspring were able to care for themselves. I do not believe it is the parents' job to care for their child/children for the duration of the parents' lives. However, there are circumstances that may require a parent to care for their child due to some form of disability. A twenty-year-old offspring, unemployed, not in college, and living in the basement should not be the expectation for the child or parent. The lack of a vision or plan for the future should not be any parent's dream for their child.

Expectations

Expectations are defined in the Oxford dictionary as a *"belief that someone will or should achieve something."*

A good task for your child is to have them define the word expectations for you or have them look up the word.

Success starts with expectations; therefore, it was expected that you would have some expectations for yourself. Remember, kids learn more from what they see than what you tell them. It is expected that you will have some expectations for your kids, and they will also have some expectations for themselves. We must have expectations for their life and share with them that there are expectations. We must help them understand that they need to have expectations as well and why. Your child should know that you are going to help them as much as possible. Especially so they can be all they have the potential to become, prompting them to achieve their dreams. Those expectations begin with them realizing that they are where they are because their parents had expectations and worked hard to get there. We as parents should expect the current position our kids are in as our offspring is the starting point for them and they are expected to do more and greater things in their lives. Additionally, they are to give back and help others as they pursue their goals. My children were taught that they had the ability to become whatever they wanted if they believed and worked hard to achieve it. And, most importantly, that prayer does work. They were also taught they would have to work twice as hard as other individuals who did not have the same skin color. My children were told this simply because there are still many people who do not believe we have the capability of achieving or that we are just as intelligent as they are, and, in some cases, more intelligent.

I often shared my upbringing on the farm with my children to reinforce the importance of their ability to achieve and appreciate education. Additionally, sharing with them the background of others who worked hard and sacrificed for us to have the benefit of becoming what we chose to be. Some of you may not want to talk to your kids about the past that we as Blacks have had to endure, but if you want your kids to be well-rounded always tell them the truth. Help them understand the struggles we and our ancestors have endured. Help them understand that they, too, will experience some of the same struggles but in a nicer and more expensive suit. Teach them that those struggles will come in many different forms and sometimes from people they thought were their friends. Also, those struggles may come from individuals who look like them but may be jealous because their parents have succeeded.

How do you help your kids learn that they need to establish expectations? Start with having expectations for yourself and let the child know that you have expectations. Help them understand that expectations are a roadmap toward creating a goal, which leads to success as long as they stay focused. Share with your child why expectations are important. Expectations are important because if you have no dreams or visions, you will never get anywhere or go far toward your potential because you will likely lack direction, along with not knowing where you are headed. Help them understand that expectations lead to desires, dreams, and result in actions. This must be passed on to your children.

Expectations cannot begin to be created when they are in high school. This is a process that starts day one. After birth, we see our child for the first time, and we want that child to look up at us and smile. As they continue to grow, we continue to have expectations for our child, whether it is our holding them by one hand, encouraging them to take that first step, or holding onto one wheel of the bicycle at the back to help them stay up on the bike. These expectations continue as we present them with flowers and ice cream after kindergarten graduation.

Some of you will secretly wish and pray that your child will make something of themselves as they grow older, but you won't express that to them. Privately, you will be hoping that they will soon find themselves and start to develop some dreams, goals, visions, or simply see themselves as a doctor, lawyer, judge, CPA, engineer, entrepreneur, etc. Parents, your child is new to life, and this is where you should guide them in some direction. Secretly hoping they will make something of themselves without any action or assistance from you will likely not help them achieve any desired dream or reach their potential. Just as you guided that bicycle and helped stabilize it so that the child would not fall off of the bike, but rather be successful and learn to ride the bike. Expectations are no different than your action of holding that bike and hoping they will learn to ride without falling. Expectations are a necessity and must be developed early in life. They can be modified or changed, but never should they be completely discarded.

Expectations should be an ongoing process, as one expectation is met others should be standing in the planning zone for execution. These expectations should also be connected to some potential goal. It is not unusual for those expectations to divert to a different direction. Don't be disheartened if they do, remember the long-term objective is to help your child achieve their potential. This can be frustrating at times as things don't always flow the way you expect they would or should. For example, my middle child initially aspired to be a pediatric cardiovascular neurosurgeon, and she certainly has the intellect for it. However, we also learned that she is quite talented in the arts. She started her college career at the Art Institute of Chicago, an impressive and highly selective institution. After we accepted the fact that she was not going to a traditional college or university and identified that the field of the Arts may be a challenge for her livelihood, I resorted to prayer that God would direct her and help her find the thing that would satisfy her and support her lifestyle. We had no doubt that she was up for the challenge and would excel.

In her first semester, she did exceptionally well as we expected. However, the second semester started in January, and the winters in Chicago are nothing to play with. Two weeks into the semester she announced she was coming home because it was too cold. Having instilled into our children that they always had to have a backup plan, the question was then what the next plan. Her plan was to return home and take some classes at the University of Louisville while she reapplied for admission to other universities. She executed her plan and, in the fall, started at the University of Southern California in Los Angeles, on a presidential scholarship. As expected, she is an extremely detail-oriented person who has calculated the number of hours she needs to graduate in four years. This action was a totally different plan from what had previously been crafted, but that road would lead to her completing a Ph.D. in sociology from the University of California Los Angeles. Plans change;

goals change but the expectation of having expectations does not. Directions may change, but your ability to support yourself successfully remains constant. This does not mean that, once they graduate, you may not ever have to assist with some financial assistance, but it should not be lifelong.

Key Take-A-Ways About Expectations

The takeaway for expectations is:
1. Make sure there are expectations; it is important that your child knows they are required to have expectations.
2. Start early in your child's life, requiring them to create expectations and make sure the expectations are relative to the child's age.
3. Discuss the expectations with your child and help them understand the needs of each expectation.
4. Require the child to engage in the process, meaning they need to do the research necessary in order to achieve that expectation or goals. In addition to being engaged, the parent must also be supportive and actively involved in setting expectations with the child.
5. Parents must also have expectations for themselves; you should not expect your child to do something you are not willing to do. Children are more likely to comply or complete something if they see or know that the parent is willing or has already done the same thing they are being asked to do.

6. Expectations should be thoroughly researched and should always have options or alternatives.
7. Expectations should always have some succeeding expectations. This means that once an expectation is near accomplishment or accomplished, there should be another expectation waiting to be started as the previous one ends.

The Road To Success Is By Determination

Another part of the road to success is determination, willpower, and the ability to move forward without having a pity party when you experience a failure or setback. Success is achievable if you are determined and willing to exert the willpower to move forward toward your dreams or goals. As a parent, this is something you will have to instill in your child as you continue to develop your own willpower and maintain your determination and drive to achieve and help your child achieve.

Determination can be taught and can be transferred from one event to another event. It can also serve as a motivating factor when you or your child is facing a daunting task that they think they cannot achieve. It may take you teaching them how to brainstorm to create a viable process to conquer the impending task. An example of this is when one of my daughters auditioned to attend a summer music program at Davidson College. Initially, she was not selected to attend the advanced class but was invited to attend a class below the advanced class. In her competitive state of mind, she was disappointed she didn't get into the top class. During our debrief on the drive home, she was encouraged to think about what she could have done differently. Her response was to practice more. I suggested that although Davidson was a highly competitive program to get into, she did have the opportunity to prove to them that they made a mistake by not offering her a spot in the top group. I continued to share with her that when she came back for the summer, she could show them her ability and potential. It would take determination, willpower, and her getting over what she felt was a failure to achieve her goal of getting into the top group. Also, it would take a lot of determination in the form of hard work. She took the bait and asked her music coach to prepare her for the summer program. She requested more challenging music pieces and sought whatever guidance she needed to follow from her music teacher. Her music teacher researched the types of music pieces that students who were studying at Davidson were playing and incorporated those into her routine lessons.

Upon her return to the start of the summer program, she performed well with the pieces assigned to her group, but the faculty noticed she had a greater skill set than what they had observed in the audition.

By the close of the program, she was invited to spend the additional week with the top group. When she called to tell me she had been asked to stay an additional week to play with the top group, I reminded her that her determination and hard work with her music teacher had helped her achieve her intended goals. It was also an opportunity to share with her that if she had not seen her initial attempt to go into the top group fail, she would not have been prepared to excel in the top group and succeed. That's not the end of the lesson; by the end of the first day in the advanced group, she called home and said I don't think I can do this. I asked why and she explained that because she had been given a large number of pieces of music to learn in three days. She continued to say she could not do it, and it was impossible to learn that much new material in a short time. I reminded her that she was determined to get into the top group and had exemplified great willpower to do what was necessary to improve her chances of getting into the top group. Now that she had joined that group, and the requirements were greater and expectations were higher for greater production, she lacked the confidence to meet the demand. I asked her a simple question, "How many notes can you play at a time?."

Consequently, I challenged her to learn one note at a time and then one stanza at a time. She tried that method and, yes, it worked. She learned all the pieces and was ready to play in the final concert.

The benefit of that experience enabled us to use it later when she felt she could not do well in her graduate professional studies. That time, she was able to think back on the prior experience, then dig deep into the barrel of willpower, and move forward with the hard work needed to be successful in her next endeavor. That experience gave her the boost in willpower to forge ahead and adjust any method of study necessary to make sure she achieved her goal.

From this point on, she has demonstrated the determination and willpower to accomplish her goals. She had learned that having a pity party over failures is not fruitful but rather an opportunity to make adjustments in the process and to inject a bolus of willpower with a desire to forge ahead toward her intended goal. These experiences have taught her to look at what most consider a failure as an opportunity for success.

Finding an event that can be a lifelong lesson is one of the most effective ways I taught my children determination and willpower. Additionally, looking at failures as an opportunity for exploration of options or opportunities to find a solution for succeeding at a different level.

Key Take-A-Ways About Determination

Some takeaways are:
1. Use real-life situations as tools to train and/or build confidence, determination, drive, and willpower.
2. Help your child actively work through those situations and preserve the pieces that can be used later in life for either similar or new challenges.
3. Teach your child to see failure not as the enemy, but as an opportunity for greater achievement and growth.

Goals

How do you get to a place where you have no idea exists? You can get there through trial and error, and by looking at the paths others have traveled, and create your own path. As the parent, it is imperative that you help your child develop goals.

Remember, the first step is to have goals for yourself. Growing up on the farm in a very small town created a very unexposed and naiveness about what else existed in the world. Never having been to a movie theater, or on a plane, ship, or a laundromat created an opportunity to learn about the world. My oldest sister had a different father and did not always stay with us. This resulted in her having more exposure to the world "off the farm," and she was a great role model for me. Her going to college signaled to me that I could also go to college.

There is something internal in each of us that becomes a natural inclination to desire to do something or be something. It is the destiny within us that brings an internal smile to our existence. It's that thing that you often think about subconsciously; it is what we were designed to become. There is nothing that guarantees that it will be easy or economical, but it is your road to happiness, self-fulfillment, and success. Learning to harness this natural and internal desire, as well as identifying it in your child or children, is part of the beginning steps to directing them toward developing goals.

We must first understand that our children are individuals and not the channel through which we can relive our life choices or correct the mistakes we made along the way. We ourselves must have a desire to see them succeed beyond what we have accomplished. (Don't be jealous if they do).

You must understand and acknowledge that sometimes you may have to travel the road alone. Also, help your child understand that they, too, may have to walk the road alone sometimes if they truly want to succeed. Depending on your career choices, job obligations will dictate the time you will be accessible to your child, which is crucial. My husband, as a doctor started his career in academic medicine and it was very time demanding. As a result I finally understood what one of my aunts once said to me many years before—

that I would be a living widow. I learned that my husband would spend almost all of his time in the hospital caring for patients, teaching students, fellows, and doing his research. When he came home, he would still work on his research in pursuit of tenure and ultimately a full professorship. This resulted in everything around the home and family being a task for me to do. When I found myself working a job that required me to be in the hospital at times at least ten or more hours a day, it was time to make a decision to find another job because we needed the income. I needed the time to invest in our children. Switching jobs to accommodate the need for a parent to be home with the kids after school and help with school-related work, meals and care for the home was not necessarily the desired thing for me to do. However, it was the thing that needed to be done.

You must be grounded in something that will help you stay grounded and focused. For me, it was my belief in Jesus Christ. If I had no one else, who I could share my frustration I could with him, and he would listen and provide me with the strength to keep climbing up the mountain. Also, faith and having a church home that you are actively involved in is also a means for which Jesus can provide valuable solutions and resources. Resources are not always financial; they can be babysitting, or a fellow member taking my son to Boy Scouts' meetings with their child while I am taking another child to tutoring or music lessons. Of course, that also means you being willing to give, which leads to your readiness to help others with their needs. The benefit of having a church home and raising your kids in that environment provides examples for you to teach your kids what to do and what not to do. What not to do because not all church folks have a relationship with Jesus and may not treat your child as you would, so you have to be careful in your selection of individuals who will have access to your child. The church can provide a solid foundation internally, which your child can build upon. It can also teach them responsibility. As I worked in the nursery on some Sundays so other parents could attend the worship service, I would often have my children working beside me so they could understand that supporting others is a part of life and contributes to their own success as well.

Do not underestimate the importance of the foundation, as you and your child will learn that many challenges will require them and you to stand on that foundation. This does not mean that one cannot be successful in the eyes of society without knowing Jesus Christ, yet the richness and depth that one can reach with Christ is beyond our imagination.

Goals must be set, but the real question is how, when, and by whom they should be established. Helping your kids set goals starts with you setting goals for yourself. Don't expect your children to do something you are not willing to do. Setting goals should be done by thoughtful and thorough observations of your child's habits, likes, dislikes, smiles, rebellious incidents, and, most importantly, listening to what the child verbalizes. This requires you as a parent to actively communicate with your child; that is, talk and listen to the child in person. My goal was to raise children who would be productive and contribute to society in a positive way. Goal setting involves more than just jotting down words; it also involves your child's passion, research, likes, dislikes, and capabilities. You must also help your child to understand that there are perimeters that they must meet and comply with for their chosen career path. If your child hates science, they probably won't become a doctor, or if they don't like math or numbers, they most likely won't become a certified public accountant. Keep in mind that a dislike can become a passion if the desire is strong enough, so don't count anything out, but allow the child to exclude it if they come to that conclusion. Also, just because a child is talented in a certain area, that alone does not mean it is the career path they should pursue. Most importantly, the child does not have to follow in your footsteps or career path.

The goals you and your child develop should first and foremost be realistic. It is utmost important to be realistic. Being realistic means understanding what you are working with, whether that is doing it alone as a single parent or absent parent, your financial resources, limitations, and environmental resources, such as the quality of the schools your child attends. Being realistic means your child may not become or take the career path you want them to take. Being realistic means, you submit to the fact that your child is a person of their own being and has likes and dislikes of their own. Being realistic about your child and their capabilities enables you to assist your child in creating realistic goals.

As a parent, our goal should always be to help our children achieve their potential. In doing so, it will require us to be the role model that they look up to and not afford them to take a substitute role model from television. Having a role model gives the child someone to look for answers, assistance, and or resources. It also allows them to see someone in a position for which they desire to become. An example of this is Dr. Serena Stoddard #6, who graduated from Tuskegee Veterinary School in May 2023, has always had a passion for animals. The process of connecting her with a veterinarian and seeking out a joint mentor for Serena was a task for me as her mother. Allowing someone to have access to your children is the responsibility of parents to thoroughly vet the person. Having observed Serena's passion and exposing her to someone I trust and who was familiar with led me to help her set one of her goals of becoming a veterinarian. Serena started in elementary school visiting our veterinarian office a few times a week. Serena would observe the veterinarian and do whatever was asked of her, even if it was to just clean the cages. Allowing her to volunteer exposed her to the possibilities while allowing her to see the realistic side of what the field of veterinarian medicine required.

The goal for Serena was set by her in conjunction with me, providing her guidance and support in any way possible. With both of us researching what it would take to become a veterinarian, we were able to develop a playbook for her to use as her guide. This process required both of us to research what it takes to get into veterinary school. Identifying those criteria at an early stage in her school days allowed us to map out a detailed plan of action. One of the goals of the research was to identify what it would take to successfully get into veterinary school. We identified that a number of service hours were required with animals and with a veterinarian, as well as their reference for the admissions applications. Additionally, the number of hours needed actually had to be proof available to verify those hours, the type of interaction with the animals, and whether a veterinarian was present. This allows us to search for specific volunteer opportunities that would allow Serena to obtain the hours as well as maximize any other benefits she could derive from the activities. This further led her to volunteer at the Louisville Humane Society. From this point on, my task was to observe her progress while she volunteered; (no I did not go with her), but rather I would have debriefed or had a conversation when I picked her up or dropped her off. These conversations would help me identify her ability to stick with this path as well as identify any potential for problem areas and success. I could also gage her passion for this career choice. Also identify if she had the skills and capability to become a veterinarian. Additionally, I identified she had great creative skills, research skills and remarkable teaching skills. I was also careful to look for teachable moments that could be used at any point in her career path, especially when she would become discouraged. With these tools she is now capable of the direct pursuit of her goal.

This will work for any career path your child wants to pursue. Therefore, the goal of becoming a veterinarian was set by serena and coached by me as her parent. This goal was set in middle school. As a parent you have to be very intuitive and in tune with observing your child and listening to what they are saying, as well as what they are doing. Believe what you see in real time they are clues that will lead you to your child's potentials and dreams. While you are observing your child, paying attention to their feelings, does the task appear to be a chore for them or is there a smile on their face? Ask yourself whether or not you have to drag them out of the house to take them to the volunteer place. Are they willing to do the task without receiving a reward or payment? Does the child talk about the places where they are volunteering with passion? Do they do their other chores with haste in order to get to the volunteer place? These are questions or observations you should be looking for to stage their true interest.

Some kids may be late bloomers, but you must not give up on them, instead you must constantly observe them and what they do. My oldest, who has great talent, had planned to follow in her father's footsteps and become a doctor. She has a passion for helping people and loves science. Her becoming a doctor seems like a good fit. However, in high school she did a research project and presented that research in competition. Her presentation skills and research skills were exceptional. She was encouraged to do more research and the next year she selected another project and won the state competition and a national science camp spot. Despite the victory of winning the science camp spot she elected not to go and chose a summer premed program at the undergraduate university she attended.

Shana had already been warned that Organic Chemistry was a weed-out course for medical school entry. Knowing this allowed her to be extra ready to take on organic chemistry. Well yes, she aced the course, but also figured out that chemistry was more interesting than becoming a doctor and was a better path for her. Don't take it personally that all the preparation you were involved in, and all the research you helped your child with—expecting it would support her chosen career—now feels wasted. Remember it is their life, and they will be the ones to get up every morning to go to whatever job they choose. Shana, figuring out she loves chemistry, and it was the best fit for her than medical school. Encouraging her to continue in chemistry still offered the option for medical school to be on the table. This pivot to chemistry created the additional need to explore new options—specifically those involving chemistry. This eventually led to Shana obtaining her PhD in chemistry. Her passion to help others was not lost as she started mentoring students at Rhodes College where she is a tenure assistant professor. Shana's mentoring focuses on students interested in entering the science, technology, engineering and mathematics (STEM) field of study. This was done by mentoring and preparing these students for graduate school or professional school. This has led to her receiving multiple international awards for mentoring along with a potential patent in chemistry. Also, this had led to Shana establishing her own company and foundation to mentor, and develop a premier program designed to promote disadvantaged individuals' greater success in the area of STEM.

Key Take-A-Ways- Goal Setting

The key takeaway for setting goals is to:
1. Be realistic,
2. Set your own goals as an example.
3. Be observative,
4. Allow the child to demonstrate their internal passion,
5. Conduct the research and include optional outlets if they change their mind.
6. Allow the child to set their own goals.
7. Debrief or constantly evaluate progress and adjust as needed.
8. Talk with your child,
9. Listen to your child.
10. Provide the support needed for your child to succeed. Support comes in many ways such as driving them to the various locations needed for them to get the exposure or experience they need.
11. Do not force your goals to be their goals. Let them live their dream and if you are not living yours go after your own.
12. Work those plans together, it is a valuable lesson they will need to be successful and survive.

Parental Observation To Identify Each Child's Capability, Identification Of Characteristics, Traits and Passions

The key to knowing your children will require you to spend time with them, "dedicated time." This cannot be delegated to anyone else. It is not the school's or the teacher's responsibility to teach you about your child. School teachers/ educators are an asset to you and your child, and to you raising your child. School/ teachers should not be the primary assessors of your child's abilities or capabilities. You must respect your child's teacher by working with them to educate your child. You must also demand that your child respect the teacher. Therefore, it is important that you be aware of your child's capabilities before they go off to school, simply by knowing what your child is capable of doing. During the years before your child goes off to school, you have the opportunity, ability, and obligation to identify the capabilities within your child. You, as the parent, should have already identified whether your child tends to persist or give up easily. Perhaps the child persists in saying "I can do it" or "I can't do that." What have you observed? Is your child regularly trying a difficult task for a child or do they take the easy toy? What does your child actually do with the toy? I did not buy many dolls for my daughters because I observed they were more interested in how to take them apart and put them back together than in playing with them. When there was a choice between a doll and the operation game, the game always won. Although my husband did not have a lot of time to spend with the kids, when he did, he would teach them how to play chess or other mind-building/thinking games. Sometimes those games were not really games but ways to stretch their minds, such as alternate squares or lava. Don't feel confused, I never heard of those either. Jumping squares or landing on certain places would result in you sinking into lava-filled holes. It is not on the market, but a creative way to teach timetables and the science of lava and its capabilities.

What kinds of books do they gravitate towards? My fourth child gravitated to books, but not just any book; she preferred books thick in size. It may have been influenced by my thick law school textbooks or my husband's thick textbooks on cardiology, such as Braunwald's textbook on heart disease.

Other ways of assessing your child's capabilities are by what they want to watch on television? What do they do in their spare time? What chores do they try to get out of doing? How do they perform those chores? The responses to these questions can tell you a lot about your child. For example, if your child does their chores meticulously with patience, care, and dedication, is that a sign of their ability to be detail-oriented, thorough, and/or precise. Those are attributes that are beneficial in certain disciplines and their fields of study, such as the field of medicine, law, engineering, etc. Another example, if the child wants to be a certified public accountant and they are not so keen on being thorough or do not like math, you may not want them to be your certified public accountant.

It is important that you, the parent, maintain control of your child and their learning opportunities. This is not a responsibility as a parent, I was willing to hand it over to any teacher, counselor, or school. If it appeared that there were adult issues or a perception that needed to be addressed with my child's teacher or the way a teacher projected my child, that issue was addressed immediately with that teacher. If that meant removing my child from a school or a particular classroom, I made sure it was well documented and addressed. An example of this is when my son was in the second grade, my son's pediatrician suggested to me that I may need to consider removing my son from the school he was in. My investigation into the situation led me to identifying that many African American males are intentionally and sometimes unintentionally labeled between the second and third grade as successful or needing to go to special education. My son's teacher at the second-grade level suggested that my son had attention deficit disorder and needed to be placed on medication. First of all, she was not a doctor, and my son's father is a doctor, although that was not his specialty. In this case, she recommended we take our son to a specific specialist for assessment of attention deficit disorder. My research on this particular individual suggested that he had a very high rate of children who had been labeled and placed on medication. We agreed, but also informed the teacher we would also have him assessed by friends at Johns Hopkins, Washington University, and King's Daughters Hospital in Virginia. To my surprise, the teacher was shocked I would even consider such an extensive assessment. As I explained to the teacher, if there was something my child needed, we would ensure he received it so he could be successful. The assessments did not come out as she expected, and my son was never placed on any medicine. The second thing she reported was that he was not on the same level as the other students and that he was disruptive in class. Unbeknownst to her, one of my sorority sisters knew the individual who trained the teachers to identify students needing assistance, including attention deficit disorder, as her specialty. I asked her to make an unscheduled visit to observe my son in school for behavior and make a recommendation to me. Her recommendation supported my decision to remove my son and daughter from that school. My son's pediatrician told me she did not like the teacher telling my son he should be a janitor, and that is what he was well-suited for as a career. Her assessment was that the teacher was destroying my son's sense of confidence in his ability to achieve by downplaying the accomplishments he was making in class and not calling on him when he raised his hand. That he was seated in the back of the room and positioned as a castaway and pretty much ignored. My son did not have a behavior problem while at school nor at home. There is nothing wrong with being a janitor if that is your child's desire, but do not allow any teacher or other school official to tell you something about your child that you know is not accurate. I knew before my son went to school, that he would not be a disruptive student because he knew the consequences and it was not his character. You will know this because you already know your child's traits, character, characteristics, passions, and behaviors because of your own parental observation. This will allow you to make the best decision for your child. If you are wondering, both children went to a different school the next school year, and my son now holds a Ph.D. in Mechanical Engineering and has never been on any medication. The decision to remove my children from that school was made with their best interests in mind. Also, this decision was made despite my daughter wanting to stay at the school, and the school wanting her to remain. For those of you who have reached a level of financial ability to pay for your child to go to private school, and or those who become benefactors of a scholarship for your child to attend it is not always a blessing. One bad teacher supported by the administration is not an option for any of my children. As the parent, I have the responsibility and right to ensure my minor child is in the appropriate environment. Additionally, you should not willingly allow your child to be used as a token or a quota, nor should you pay for your child to be subjected to inadvertent abuse. This will require you to expand the need to ensure they will still receive the education and training needed to be successful in life. This can be accomplished through extra tutoring, or advanced tutoring, and summer camps using the same money you would have paid for the private school. Some of the summer camps also provided scholarships for talented students from low-income families.

Another example of identifying my child's interest was, my son initially spoke about developing an artificial heart. He would often say he was going to also be a surgeon and put the heart in himself and keep all the money. You may think this statement is kind of cute from a child, but dissect the statement. Developing anything suggests a creative, explorative, and inquisitive mindset. My son also attended a program when he was in high school called the Governor's Scholar Program during the summer. During this program, his group was assigned to make a bird-house for a swamp-like area. My son would call me and talk about the assignment, and I could hear the excitement in his voice. A few days later, he called and said he had been given the task of foreman, and he would proceed to describe the method and materials, the design he would use to build this bird-house. Having been raised on a farm and having so many brothers, I was familiar with building fences. Additionally, I had watched and helped my sibling fix things. I knew enough to ask him questions as to how he would do certain things that would fill any holes he may not have thought of for his project. This experience suggested to me that my son has the mentality to design, create, build, and analyze, and that he found great joy and excitement in doing such things. It also identified that he enjoyed the mechanics of building the bird-house.

Another example of identifying my child's potential was that my son would sit at the dinner table and slice gummy bears. Now this may seem to be an insufficient act, but I had never seen anyone slice gummy bears and substitute different colors from different gummy bears, creating a new gummy bear that was precisely the same size as the original. This identified he was visionary, has patience, has the ability to be precise, has creativity, and is determined.

Again, there are traits that are very beneficial for the field of engineering.

These examples are everyday activities that help me identify my children's capabilities. Additionally, to identify the various characteristics, traits, and passions within each of them. This valuable information will enable me to assist them in selecting a career path as well as motivating them to succeed in whatever endeavor they choose.

As a parent, you should know when to let go of the strings of your child's independence. In my experience, I believe and have noticed that allowing your child to become independent is a necessity for their growth as an adult. You should allow them to make their own mistakes, help them see the consequences of their decision, and help them learn from their decisions.

The release of strings to independence does not have to be done all at once. As your child matures, you should gauge how much independence to allow them. As a parent, you should be teaching them independence. This task can be done using everyday living issues to teach and evaluate the progress for independence.

Some examples of releasing the strings and promoting independence are through the selection of clothing to wear to school. One of my children would mix and match to create an outfit to wear the next day. This task achieved such things as ensuring they were presentable in their choices and that the choice was appropriate for school. In some cases, you may have to concede to the child's choice as a bonus that you can use later. Another one of my daughters liked to wear mix-and-match socks intentionally. Under normal circumstances, I would say no, but allowing this would give me a brownie point that I could use later when a top was too short. It is also important to understand why she wanted to wear mismatched socks. This is the same daughter who would dress the dolls. This was her creativity, and a safe way for her to further develop her talents.

The fact that she has a creative tendency allowed a safe way for her to develop an outlet for stress, especially in her high-demand chosen career. See figure 5. The picture is a large flower made of duct tape. This was a gift given to me by- my daughter. She created the design and made the flower. Another craft she does is felting.

Some examples are in Figure 1-5.

Figure 1 - Tigger a tiger created by Dr. Serena Stoddard a graduate of University of Missouri whose mascot is a tiger.

Figure 2 - Dr. Serena Stoddard the Red Panda

Figure 3 - Dr. Serena Stoddard this is a Tapir: gift made for a mentor during her internship at Colorado State University.

Figure 4 - The Rooster created by Dr. Serena Stoddard

Using her free time for such activities will always be a better choice than being in the streets or a club, and offer greater relaxation than clubbing.

Another example is to guide them to the best decision. I always encouraged my children to help others. One of my son's classmates, a female, wanted my son to help her move in the middle of the night, which also happened to be in an area of town that was not safe. My son asked if he could go. I asked him why she was moving in the middle of the night; why wasn't she moving in the daylight hours when the view of what you was doing was better; also, since she was a student, where were her parents, and was it not their responsibility to facilitate the move. Asking a series of questions is an opportunity to teach your child to make the best knowledgeable, and most logical decision. This is a skill that they will be able to use for the rest of their life. Additionally, when they go off to college you can have some sense of relief that your child has a process to use to make decisions. This process will help them analyze methodically to achieve the best possible outcome. Through these series of questions and others my son came to the conclusion that it was likely a trap to something bad, so he chose not to go.

Take Away From Parental Observation

Take away from parental observation of each child's capability, identify characteristics, traits, and passions. The greatest benefit is that you getting the following:

1. To spend quality beneficial time with your child and develop a lifelong relationship.
2. Knowing your child allows you the ability to help direct them down a certain exploratory path of potential careers.
3. A potential guide to explore options for career choices, summer camps, enrichment programs, and other things that will help your child succeed.
4. Open the opportunity for you to have valuable and productive conversations with your child's teachers and counselors.
5. Cost-saving prevents parents from wasting money on things such as piano lessons when there is absolutely no interest in the piano.
6. Don't be afraid to make the tough and unpleasant but necessary decisions for the benefit of your child and their future.
7. Be the parent you created and give birth to or adopt that child, it's your responsibility.

Figure 5: Flower made of duct tape, a mother's day gift by Dr. Serena Stoddard

Figure 6: Praying Mantis made of scrap fabric by Dr. Carmella Stoddard

Figure 7: Graduation gift to Dr. Carmella Stoddard upon completion of undergraduate studies at the University of Southern California, from her sister Dr. Erica Stoddard

Parenting

As the parent, you gave birth to your child, or you chose to adopt the child, therefore, it is your responsibility to be the parent. You are not your child's friend, not now, not ever. You are the parent, so be the parent. There are cases where due to circumstances, you now have your grandchild, nephew, sibling, or niece; regardless of the circumstances, they are now under your leadership. The keyword is you; it is your responsibility to raise, train, guide, lead, and protect your child. You have the authority to do so. This is not an area you should delegate to someone else to direct or do without your close supervision.

Parenting is not the same as it was when my mother raised me. The courts didn't care if you received a whipping with a belt or if you were old enough to remember a switch from the peach tree. Children didn't talk back to parents, and there was a respectful fear that parents ruled the house and the children within and outside that house. If you are from a small town or the country, then the whole community has the right to correct you when you step outside the expected compliance of the household rules or act with disobedience or indifference while at school. Schools were different, and the principal did have a paddle and would use it if necessary to keep a child in line so all students could learn undisturbed. My children were raised in old school; if a punishment was warranted, it was issued. I learned early in my child rearing that if you applied the appropriate correction action early in your child's life you likely won't have to continue it because they knew that there were boundaries and if those boundaries were crossed then they would suffer the consequences of that action.

The need for discipline can be minimized, if early in the child's, life you have talked to them about acceptable and unacceptable behaviors. Also you have had previous discussions as to the consequences of certain actions they may choose. Family discussion concerning why an older child is on punishment or why they are receiving a punishment can divert the same or similar action in your younger child. Parents should always think carefully about the type and timing of discipline they issue to a child.

Discipline can be minimized if you take the time explaining to the child why something is not appropriate or dangerous. Your child's receptiveness to this method is impacted by the amount of time you have spent with the child prior to the need to issue discipline. Discipline must be appropriate and timely, to be effective, and should always be purposeful. This is not an opportunity for any parent to take out their frustration with what happens on the job, or being upset with your spouse or the children. Discipline can and should be different for different children; time out has little or no effect on a child who likes to hang out in their room alone or is an introvert. Time out with no direction or explanation is of little use. If the child is able to sit in a time out and watch everything going on in the room, it may not be as effective, as when the child is in a secluded place. The type of discipline for a child is one that has to have a valuable impact. As the parent, you must demand that your child fully respect you as the parent and other adults. Also, they are willing to comply with the rules of the house and your instructions that are designed to help them achieve their fullest potential.

As the parent, you must invest in your child and in their future while they are at home. This investment must include the child's ability to survive and thrive when they are no longer living under your roof. Basic things such as cooking, cleaning, laundry, money management, studying, time management, and personal care and life management. These basic needs should be developed prior to your child going off to camp and ultimately to college.

As the parent, you are always required to be the example; don't expect your child to be something you are not willing to do or be. People who come into contact with me and my children often comment on how well-mannered and respectful my children are. That which you see in my children is a direct result of how they were raised. If you ever have the opportunity to come in contact with any of my children, not only will you be impressed, but you will be met with respect and dignity. I cannot account for any unhealthy habits they may have picked up later in life, or as they may have come in contact with someone else's child with a different upbringing. Thus far as I have had the opportunity to be exposed to other individuals my children have contact with whether from college or on the job, I am often met with "I wanted to meet you" or "I am so impressed with what you have done with your family" and the usual question "how did you do it" referring to raising five children and all becoming successful. Again, the result of a lot of prayer, sacrifice, and hard work. I have experienced a situation when visiting one of my children at their job with their coworker literally dropping what they were doing to come meet me. Many want to have a conversation as to how I did it. I have had people make requests or offer to help raise their children. One of my fellow church members shared with me that he instructed his children to sit by my children so something would rub off on them, admirable but, unfortunately, it doesn't work that way. These comments and actions are the result of the experiences and exposure these individuals have had with my children, and how my children presented themselves. With all this being said, my children are not perfect, and neither am I, but my children remember their upbringing and understanding that their name and reputation is the only thing that will last forever. I too remember my upbringing and as my mother would, say it's your name and reputation, and I was known as a "Whitlock." We were poor but highly respected in my hometown. As I went out into the world, I carried that with me and always lived up to the expectation of being a Whitlock.

Parenting has stages, which you will come to understand and must recognize. Your child will rely on you initially for their guidance, then you will have interference from their friends, college mates, coworkers, social relationships, and spouses. It is important for you as parents to know how to maneuver through those various stages. If you, as the parent, have incorporated strong values into your child during earlier years, they will likely continue to comply with their upbring.

During the school years, there may be interference by their friends and possibly the interaction of their friends' parents. This is one reason why it is important to have an impact on who your child's friends are. In some cases, where there is liberal parenting of their friends, it is a good reason not to allow your child to spend a lot of their free time with a person whose values are not the same. Additionally, many of my children's friends were not the same color, and it was my duty to constantly remind them that they might be hanging out with them, but if trouble should arise, it is likely they would be blamed for it, because of the color of their skin. They were told this because one it is a reality, and two to help them think about whether or not they wanted to take the chance of being blamed for something they might not have done. This also helped them make better decisions about who they would have as a friend. An example of this was one of my daughters had a friend whom she considered to be her best friend. My daughter severed the friendship and did not tell me about it. I noticed she stopped talking about this friend and was no longer interested in spending any time with her. Naturally, as the parent, I inquired as to what was going on with her friend. She responded that she is not my friend. I inquired about what happened to change the friendship. My daughter said her ex-friend had been drunk on alcohol. This was an elementary school fifth-grade student. I then told my daughter I was sorry she lost her best friend and proud of her for making the decision to sever the relationship. I went on to tell her I know that was a difficult and hard decision. I ask her why her decision ends the friendship instead of helping her friend make changes in her actions. To my surprise, my daughter said, "I don't have time for that, and she shouldn't be stupid drinking." From this, I learned that my daughter has a very low tolerance for people wasting their lives or living without direction. I admit I felt sorry for her friend because the road she was headed down would certainly lead to her with a shortened life or an unhappy life. As parents, we must teach our children to make tough decisions, even if it is not a popular decision and one that will be painful for them.

Another example is my son, who graduated from college during the time when the country was headed into a recession and companies were laying off employees. His job search during the months leading up to college graduation was not fruitful, and as a result, after graduating from college, he did not have a job. I asked him what his plans were. He responded, "Keep looking for a job and pray something would come through because he wanted to marry his girlfriend." He asked if he could come home while he searched for a job so he would not have to pay rent on an apartment. His girlfriend, at the time, wanted him to stay in the area, and because he had enough money from his saving and graduation gifts he could afford it. However, my son made the decision that he would come home to live rent-free for the six-month time period I had given him as long as he was looking for a job and had an alternate plan. Please note my policy was if you are trying to improve or advance yourself, we would do what we could to support, but that was not a retirement plan. Therefore, he could come home as long as he had a plan, and we would support him as much as we could. During that time, he participated in the household chores, including transporting his siblings to school.

My son came home, and the relationship with his girlfriend at some point came to an end because she wanted to get married, and he was not ready. He was devastated. As we discussed the situation, he shared that I had always told him that "before you think about getting married, he needed to have three things, a job, health insurance, and a place to put his wife. Now, concerning the place to put his wife, it is my belief that two women cannot run the same house. Additionally, every woman has the right to take care of her own husband; it is not my job to take care of any woman's husband. Also, the job would provide a steady income to care for his family, and health insurance needs no explanation. I was happy my son remembered that teaching and made the decision he made. This was a painful decision for my son, but he made it on his own. As the parent it was now my task to help him through the lack of a job, loss of the woman he loves, and identifying an alternate plan if he was not able to find a job in six months. During this time, he worked hard to find a job, but by month three, there was not a job in sight, so he decided to also apply for graduate programs as an alternative. His sister was at the University of Mississippi doing well, so naturally, he started there. She had just won a recognition to attend the Lindau Nobel Laureate Meeting to hang out with Nobel prize winners, which is by invitation only, and the university was excited to now have a student represent them at such a prestigious international level. The entire university was made aware of the distinction. To my daughter's credit as she always looks out for her siblings, she stopped by the engineering school and told them her brother wanted to work on his PhD. He applied and was offered a position to start in January (in two months) of the upcoming year with all fees paid and a stipend. A few days later, he received his first job offer, which paid the same as the stipend he would have received if he went to school. He now had a choice to go to work for a job that was clearly paying him less than an individual with a degree in mechanical engineering should have been paid, or go to graduate school. He chose graduate school because he had been taught about delayed gratification. I ask him to research what the average income for someone with his credentials should be and do his pro/con for the job or school, and then make his decision. Of course, one of his pros for the job was that he could then go back after the woman he loved and wanted to marry, and because of delayed gratification he knew to look long-term. He had the tool for making his own, and the best decision for him. He has since graduated with his PhD in Mechanical engineering and has made multiple times more than he would have if he had accepted the low-paying job. Now he has his dream job and the woman he loves as his wife, the same girl as before. It was a painful decision but a fruitful one.

Parenting will sometimes require you to make calculated decisions about everything you do for your children. Sometimes, allowing them to fail will provide a lifelong learned lesson. These kinds of decisions can only accurately be made if you know your child, which means you have spent the time getting to know how far your child will go. As the parent, you must selectively choose when and in which situation to use to teach that lifelong lesson. An example of such is one of my daughters decided to play around in class with her best friend instead of doing her schoolwork. Earlier, I mentioned that you should know all your children's teachers and have a presence in the school where your child attends so much so that the teacher will personally contact you and inform you what is going on. One of my daughter's teachers shares with me that my daughter is playing with her best friend in class, and as a result, her grade is falling. She was turning in her homework but not doing anything beyond that. As the teacher shared with me, her grade had fallen from an A to a C, and if her behavior persisted, she would earn the grade of a D for the semester. This is a case where parental intervention is a must. To protect the teacher-parent relationship, I did not share the information with my daughter, instead I researched through the school policy what would happen if a student received an F in a course. I identified that if a student fails a class, they could take it over the summer, and the school would replace the F with the grade achieved over the summer. I asked the teacher to give her no extra credit, accept no late assignments, and give her no benefit of the doubt, and if she was anywhere near anything other than what the teacher thought was her potential, she deserved an F. When my daughter came home with a C for math in her midterm grade, I immediately told her it looked like she could benefit from some tutoring. I signed her up for tutoring with a math specialist who did 4 sessions with her. I was then told not to bring her back because based upon her assessment, my daughter was advanced in math and did not need tutoring, but needed to be challenged at a higher level than what she was taking in school. I was happy to save that money. Nevertheless, I had to develop an alternate plan of options to teach her a lesson as well as preserve her GPA. I met with the school counselor and had her remove my daughter from any future classes with her best friend and keep the two separated in all future classes. I also had additional conversations with the counselor as to what class she could take over the summer that could replace the class she was going to fail. We selected an appropriate replacement class, and the teacher was going to give her the grade she deserved in the math class. When the semester ended, and she received an F in a class even though she was very capable of making an A in. She was devastated by the fact that she had to bring home the grade as an "F" when she knew she was capable of doing the work. No child of mine had ever brought home an F grade; it was unacceptable. I asked my daughter what she was going to do about it. Through the tears, she was lost as to what to do. Time for my plan of lifelong learning lessons, also known as summer school. I shared with my daughter that she was going to go to summer school in order to replace the F she had earned. In addition, she would have to pay for it as well and pay me for having to take her to class. She would lose her opportunity to attend any summer camps and was on punishment until she earned an appropriate grade. I then immediately took her to the place where she needed to register for the summer class. I informed her that since she had to go to summer school, she may as well make the most out of it. Since she was having to go to summer school for a class she could have passed with an A and lose her summer enrichment activities, she may as well sign up for additional classes because she had no other privileges that she would be doing that summer. After she signed up for classes, we proceeded to McDonald's so she could get a job to pay for the classes. I had previously spoken to a friend who owned the McDonald's about hiring her for the summer to pay for the classes she would be taking during the summer. I had shared with this friend what was going on and the lesson she needed to learn. The lesson for her to learn was that she could use her brains or her hands to make a living; the choice was up to her. My daughter attended summer school and took three classes, including math, and made an A in all classes. She also did not enjoy working at McDonald's, and that was a lesson well learned. During that class, she met some very different students who eventually asked her why she was there since it was obvious to them that she was smart and knew the math. This gave her something to think about as to why she had wasted a semester playing around in a class she could have easily aced.

When the next school term started on the first day, I picked her up from school and she informed me she had no classes with her best friend and wasn't sure why. I then told her they could see each other during lunch or after school. I did not tell her I had made those arrangements or that they would never have a class together again. Well, I saw no reason to tell her I had requested that she and her best friend not be in any more classes together. She will learn it when she reads this book.

Other people who can influence your children are the people they have romantic relationships with. As the parent, you will have to safeguard your child in these intimate relationships that you may think or know are not the best for them. As the loving parent, you will want to put a stop to those relationships and, in most cases, help them see they need to get rid of that unlikely choice of a potential mate. They may not like it, but as I was used to saying "who cares" because what is best for them is still what you want for them as a parent. Some examples are any girl who sent my son an inappropriate birthday card such as one with a women's breast on it, it's a clear no.

If a young man is two years older than my daughter and has finished high school and had no plans for, college even though he had funding available and free of charge for him to attend, and he chooses not to go, it is a no. One of my daughters once told me before she brought the young man home that she really needed me to like this guy. This comment did what most parents think our words to our kids do: "in one ear out the other." When the young man came to visit, I asked him what his plans were for the future, and he responded with something like he was trying to save up $2,000 to buy a motorcycle. Wrong answer, and he was not a keeper. I later shared with my daughter and reminded her of her plans for life and how his goals can intertwine with what she wants to do in life. I asked her to look at what he would have to offer as assistance and or support for her achieving her goal versus what she has to offer him for him to achieve his goal. Being that she was in high school and had saved all of her money for good grades, she had enough to give him to buy a motorcycle. I reminded her that she had enough money to give him $2,000 for the obviously used motorcycle and asked her then what his plan was. This was inviting her to think through that relationship and what potential it had for her to succeed. She later invited him back to visit and told him it wouldn't work. She came to that conclusion on her own, and it was the correct one. I imagined she remembered how hard she had worked for that money, for good grades, and wasn't about to give it to someone who had no other goals.

Sometimes we as parents have to make really tough, painful decisions that fit the disobedience. One of my children decided to take a trip with her friends and not ask permission or tell her parents. I am sure she knew if she asked, she would have received a no. Therefore, she was going to accept whatever punishment she would be given. She was gone for the weekend leaving only one one-line text message on the phone I will be back on Sunday. Of course, I thought this girl had lost her mind. All the doors were locked, and she could not get into the house even through the passcode door unless she woke one of us up, when she called, I open the door and told her to get in the car, I took her to the red roof inn hotel and paid for a week stay and told her to figure it out from there. She was told she was welcome to come back home if she was willing to follow the rules. The week went by, and she didn't come home; instead, she went to the boyfriend's mother's house. I constantly prayed for her and solicited prayers from two of my sisters as well. I would visit her and offer for her to come home once or twice during that time she was gone, with the same restrictions following the household rules. Prayer works she eventually came home at the urging of the boyfriend's mother, who told her she was being stupid for hanging out with her "deadbeat" son who had no vision or goals for his future and was living in his mom's basement, except to play in a band. She told her she did not understand why she would waste her life with someone who is not going, anywhere while she had parents who were willing and supportive of her to achieve her potential. My daughter did come home, and we did not have any further issues with her making reckless choices. The decision to kick her out was one of the most painful decisions for me as a mom, and one that was risky, but one that I firmly believe prayers would see me through it and make the difference in the outcome. I found my strength in prayer and fasting to get me through this period of rebellion. This doesn't mean I did not shed many tears; I did, but my action was necessary to get her back on track and to make sure none of her younger siblings ever thought about any such crazy idea. My husband did not like the idea, but the one thing he was great at doing was allowing me to make the best decision I could for the future of our children, and he supported those decisions.

Making tough decisions, decisions that need to be made, regardless of how painful those decisions are, should be made for the best interest of the individual child and their potential capabilities in life. You will eventually get over the hurt once the situation is resolved. I must admit, I do not know if I could have made the same decision, if I did not have a strong prayer life and believe that my God would answer my prayer. Also, I would be very leery about making a decision without someone to lean on for support. I can only thank God that the situation turned out as it did, and she is now one of Dr. Stoddard's and has a brilliant mind.

Parenting does not end when they graduate from high school or even college. Children who desire to continue their education to the doctorate or professional level will also meet with challenges as they continue to move forward. Minority children will have an additional challenge in that there may not be anyone who looks like them in their class. Her friends may not understand the challenges of a doctoral program, and neither will some boyfriends. One of my children felt guilty because she could not spend much time with her boyfriend, and the relationship eventually ended. She has stayed focused on getting to her dream job and is doing what she needs to achieve that goal. She is gorgeous, and she will get another man who can appreciate her beauty and brilliant mind. There will be times when, as a parent, you may need to do a wellness check on your child as they try to achieve their dream. If you have spent time observing them as they grew up and identified when they reach a point of overwhelming frustration, and you need to provide physical support in any way possible, you must do so. I have had to do that on multiple occasions. All graduate schools are challenging, and helping your child realize that they may need to change their study style or reminding them that graduate school or professional school is not like going to college, just like going to college is nothing like high school, and they need to adjust accordingly to the field of study they are pursuing. Taking the time to take them out to eat or clean their apartment, cook a few meals, go to a movie, or just listen to what they are being challenged with and offering suggestions may be the significant injection they need to continue on. Regardless of which you choose, please don't hesitate to go and visit or check up on your child. This means you will need to have regular conversations to know what is going on with them and maintain a keen sense of parental observation and the need for physical intervention.

Earlier, I mentioned, don't expect your child to do something you are not willing to do. The purpose is it is easier to motivate them if they see that you have done it or are doing something similar to what they are trying to achieve. Additionally, you will have some understanding of what they will be facing and can use that as a method of encouragement for them.

Takeaway From Parenting

Parenting takeaways are:
1. Be the parent.
2. Make a decision at an early stage, but then transition to what I call exploratory decision making. This is a process where you ask the questions that will help your child make the right decision.
3. Know when to identify the lifelong teachable moments that will benefit your child.
4. Always remember each child is an individual and, as such, will be motivated by different things.
5. Do your research to address challenges your child may face.
6. Allow your child to make the final decision, but make sure they understand the options and consequences of all the options.
7. Never let a teachable moment pass without making the best of it to benefit your child.
8. Don't be afraid to make calculated, tough decisions. They will be painful to all parties involved.
9. Teach your children delayed gratification.

10. Teach your child how to do a SWOT(strengths, weaknesses, opportunities, threats) analysis when they make any tough decision.

Emotions, Environmental Factors, and Effects

There are many factors, such as environmental, internal, external, emotional, and intimate relationships that can affect the ability to raise successful children. The environmental factors are things such as other people, places, video games, YouTube, TikTok, coaches, dance instructors, or any type of teacher or instructor. These can either negatively or positively effects, and depending on the relationship you have with these people, they can become influential assistants to you. There will come a time in your child's life when nothing you say or do makes sense, but whatever the coach says is pure gospel. Having a great relationship with the coach will allow them to become a conduit for your messages and or values to be transferred to your child. This is effective if you have a supportive relationship with the teacher or coach. Your task is to identify that person you can trust to transfer your messages and teaching to your child.

Your task is to maintain control over these and the impact it will have on what you are trying to help your child become. In our home, we did not have video games, so our children did not spend all day and/ or night playing video games. We did have chess boards, Monopoly, Connect and other board games that could be enjoyed. There were no phone landlines in the children's rooms. There were no cell phones in their younger years. In today's society, almost every kid has a cellphone, and most homework is done on the computer. The safeguard to you as a parent is to allow the child to have the cell phone when outside of the home, but upon returning to home, those phones should be placed in a visible location and not in the child's room. This will eliminate the opportunity for the child to stay on the phone all night when they should be getting their much-needed rest. This does not prevent the child from using the phone to have a conversation with a friend or call a friend about an assignment.

One Internal factor that can impact child-rearing success is your emotional status as well as your child's emotional status. This is an area you should always be keen on through observation. If your child seems to be overwhelmed with schoolwork or extracurricular activities, it is your responsibility to seek a resolution. As the parent, you should always be observant of how you and/or your children are doing emotionally. Take every step to make sure each of you are emotionally stable, if not get help. If the child seems to be unhappy with an extracurricular activity, reassess what is going on and determine whether they should continue that activity. Pay attention to changes in behavior, such as attitude, sleep patterns, eating patterns, and other behaviors out of the norm. This can be a precursor to the need for change.

Monitoring emotional status is not just for the child, it is also for you as the parent. As a parent who is giving to everyone in the house and maybe also working all day, it can leave you drained and emotionally in a negative state. It is important for you as the parent to know how to release your internal bubbling over stress or burnout. Get help if you need someone to talk to. It is important for you to know what is effective for you as a stress relief factor. The squish ball may not work for you and could become a weapon thrown at someone. My stress relief is going to the movies. It doesn't matter which movie, or if it was one that I repeated. The objective was not to do anything for anyone or think about anything and eat my popcorn and drink my soda. This worked for me to refresh me to bring about a break in the daily routine and a break in the feeling of overwhelm and overburdened stress of doing everything for everybody in the house.

Intimate relationships can also be stressful and can create negativity that can cause negative impacts on your desire to raise your kids to be successful. If married, both parents have to be on the same page, or one needs to be the lead person to be in control of child rearing. Since my husband was in the hospital most of the time, this worked out best for me to assume the lead in child rearing. It was stressful at times, and there was burnout from always giving to everyone in the house and no one giving to me. This is where the movies came into play, where I didn't have to do anything for anyone. Be careful to make sure that the children spend some time with the other parents. The other parent should not be made to feel that they are not fulfilling their part of the family obligations. If they are contributing anything, then they are participating. It is important to recognize what their capabilities and limitations are and incorporate them into the process. If their capability is only to teach the kids chess, then let chess be the activity assigned while you go to the movies. Be careful not to allow jealousy or the feeling of I am in this alone or why do I have to do everything? Do not allow jealousy to take control and derail you.

Resources

You are probably thinking, a doctor and a dietitian turn lawyer, they are probably making a lot of money. Let me correct you, academic physicians for the hours they work are probably making a little more than minimum wage. Dietitians are also not a high-paying job, but a rewarding one. This being reality means you have to budget with priorities. We didn't drive the high-end luxury car, a Ford and Pontiac worked just fine, eventually a Toyota. We didn't buy the big house in the high-end neighborhood, but we did get one that met the family's needs and most importantly it was located in the best school district. The important factor to know concerning resources is to make the best decision on the utilization of those resources. In addition, you must keep in mind that everyday living and expenses exist and have to be respected.

How you utilize your financial resources is up to you, but it is important that you make the most of those resources. Being raised on a farm, I learned to cook, so we didn't eat out except for special occasions, and then only at cost-effective places. I learned to sew and made most of my kids' clothes. I would also purchase clothes off-season and catch the clearance sales. Handing down clothes with a little modification made some clothes a new design statement. I knew how to cut the grass and taught my kids as well. I did not have a cleaning company to clean our home, so we used it as a family enrichment and training activity. It was encouraging yet disturbing when my son called home from college and talked about how some of the ladies at the laundromat did not know how to do laundry. Knowing such things as you cannot wash all your clothes together and expect the white clothes to stay white should be taught at home before they go off to college. All of these were cost-saving activities. Additionally, these are necessities of life that need to be addressed regularly. The objective is to do these life necessities efficiently and cost-effectively. Keep in mind, time is also as valuable as the resources expended on it.

If you have a plethora of resources and can afford to provide the high-end for your kids. Consider not providing them with everything on their want list. They really just want to know they are loved. So seriously consider not giving them everything they speak of because things must have value and meaning. Teach them to appreciate what you work hard for and help them to know they have to work for what they get in life on their own. It is better to teach this to them and will help you help them. There's an old saying, "teach people how to fish and not just give them fish for dinner." A fish for dinner is only good for one meal, but knowing how to fish will teach them how to survive, and they can eat for a lifetime. Unfortunately, we have a new generation of individuals who feel entitled because they were provided with everything growing up, sometimes at the expense of their parents going into significant debt for it. Keep in mind that those credit card purchases will eventually have to be paid.

On the other hand, if your resources are limited, your children can still be successful using the same tools. Many summer camps offer scholarships, and the library has all the books your child may need to be successful. Discount bookstores have some of the same books as the regular bookstores. My kid's favorite place was Barnes and Noble, especially since it was within walking distance to the store from our home. Barnes and Noble have very comfortable chairs and you could preview books. Additionally, they have a café, where I often see individuals reading or pre-reading books. You will be able to look at scholarship books, standardized testing books, and books on getting into college, and other books on available scholarship information. Also, the school counselor will have access to potential local scholarship, and potential universities your child may be interested in attending to identify scholarships.

Take Away For Resources

1. Wisely use your resources. Resources, limited or not, should be routed to a specific objective or goal. The resources do not have to be equalized among your children. Having a lot of money is no guarantee that your child will achieve success. The most important factor is to enhance that child's ability to succeed. Additionally, the resources should be directed to improve or promote each child's ability to succeed. For example, math tutoring may be more beneficial for a potential engineering major than dance lessons.
2. Teach your children to utilize and respect the resources available to them. Teaching them to utilize resources will ensure they are able to make the most of their own resources as well as eventually reduce your need to support them, which should be your goal. They should not have an expectation of living in your basement for life.
3. Teach them to identify the best value for their resources, such as off-season shopping, and carefully research before purchasing.
4. Teach them about the use of credit cards and that they have to be paid back with interest.

5. Help them understand the value of a great credit score.
6. Help them to always have a savings plan, and that rainy days will come, and they will need new tires eventually.

Preparation for College

College research should start as early as the eighth (8th) eighth grade in middle school. My children were required to have a list of potential colleges no later than entry into ninth grade. The rule was they had to have a minimum of ten (10) schools to apply to on the last day of school or by the time they were entering the ninth grade. I know this is early, but here is the benefit. If you and your child know the potential school, they plan to attend, then plans can be established to evaluate and pursue admission and scholarship as well.

With this list of schools identified, your child is now able to (1) *Pull the potential essay questions from those schools as practice essay.* These essays can be used as potential essays in some of their high school classes. Help your child keep up with those essays so when they apply to those universities, they will only need to edit that essay. If they are lucky, they may have had the benefit of their high school ENGLISH teacher already having critiqued that essay. This is a time saving tool if used appropriately. I noticed the essays at the universities of interest did not have significant change in their descriptive content therefore they can edit or update those already written essays instead of starting from ground zero. (2) *Identify what it is going to take to help your child be competitive* for entry into their college or university of choice. This will require you to do some research on the schools of interest. Thoroughly reviewing the potentials institutions statistics to identify the average ACT/SAT of the upper 25 percent of admitted students score. Which standardized exam does the school prefer?

What are the other requirements necessary to be competitive for that institution? If your child is interested in going to medical/ veterinary school, one piece of information that you should identify from potential universities is the percentage of students they are able to get admitted to medical school or veterinary school. Let's take veterinary school There are approximately thirty-two veterinary schools in the United States that are accredited or pending accreditation according to the American Association of Veterinary Medical Colleges. This association also states that the acceptance rate for admission to veterinary school is only 10 percent of those who apply. The Annual data Report for the American Association of Veterinary Medical Colleges reports that there were 10,253 applications for admission with 3,860 admitted. If you are a minority the incoming class for 2025 has approximately 30 percent of the incoming class as minorities. This percentages of non-white included all categories, with approximately fifteen percent of the class male. This report also shows a median indebtedness of approximately $175,000.00 to $400,00.00. Due to research, pre-planning and sacrifice allowed my daughter to graduate with zero debt. It can be done. Also preplanning will provide potential scholarships that are germane to that institution and the criteria necessary to be a competitive candidate for that institution's scholarships.

If your child is interested in veterinary school, you will need to identify other criteria that will make them competitive for that ten percent that get admitted. Research during the summer before my daughter started high school identified what it would take to get into veterinary school. We identified that she needed to have so many hours of actual experience with animals and with an actual veterinarian. This led us to talk with our veterinarian and see if she would allow her to shadow her. We contacted the local humane society for volunteer opportunities. The average suggested volunteer hours were a minimum of 500 hours. You also had to identify what was done and whether or not there was a veterinarian present. Serena had approximately 10,000 hours of contact. Remember those summer programs, this is where we would send her to summer camp at Cub Creek Science camp in Missouri. She went every summer for two to six weeks. While there she was also able to work with their veterinarian and work her way up to a leadership role. Serena continued even after entering college where she actually obtained a summer job at the camp with pay.

Identify potential scholarships that your child may qualify for at each institution. Now that you are aware of the criteria for those scholarships you and your child can focus on meeting those criteria. It can be too late and a limitation to try and meet the criteria when your child is applying for those institutional germane scholarships at the end of the eleventh grade or beginning of the twelfth grade. Early research allowed us to create a chart to identify potential scholarships that your child would be applying for. My chart includes such things as identify application deadline, criteria/qualification, potential essay needed, scholarship specific criteria, the scholarship amount, essay criteria, and possible topic (this needed to be updated each year for changes). Another benefit is your child will be able to enjoy some of their senior year as a senior without spending all of their time on scholarship funds or writing essays. Don't be fooled, this is a tedious task and very time-consuming, but as a result all five of my children were able to graduate debt free with either their Ph.D., DVM, or MD degree. I did this for all five of the children, and yes you will have to do some of this yourself.

This is very crucial in order to assist your child in getting to their desired goal. (4) *give your kids smart gifts and incentives to perform well in school.* It will also help them to develop a great habit of working hard when they go off to college and are on their own. This teaches them that hard work does pay off and or has its rewards. Some of the incentives we had for our children were if they got all A's for the semester they would receive 100.00 cash. They had the child bank accounts at the credit union and once you put the money in the account, they could not get it out until they turned eighteen. I know, it was sneaky because it was simply adding to their college funds. Nevertheless, it afforded them the opportunity to learn how to save and deposit money in the bank. Once they turned eighteen, I would take them to the credit union and they could order their checks, picking out their own check design and then give them that checkbook with their name on it. We also had an incentive that for graduation their present was cash which was calculated based on their final GPA times 1000. Now on a four-point zero system the highest GPA you can get is a four- zero point, until the system was changed causing one child to earn $4,500, as a graduation gift. That incentive was only good for their final GPA from high school. This meant I would need to set aside a separate account money to make those payments to that child for their hard work. Each child had different incentives because each was motivated by different things. They were interested in different areas for careers which would cause them to have to work hard in school such as medical school and veterinary school. This does not mean obtaining a

Ph.D. in Chemistry, Mechanical Engineering and Sociology was less demanding. All Ph.D.'s are demanding, especially if you are doing first impression research. We also had to have multiple incentives for each child. My husband came up with the brilliant idea to challenge one of our children and offer her an incentive that if she got a four-point zero for the semester she could select any restaurant she wanted to and order anything she wanted. It was a good incentive but, in my opinion, not for that child, although my husband never knew that was my view, that particular child loved to eat and love meat. I had never been to Ruth's Chris until the end of that school year. She did receive a 4.0 at the university that semester while she was in high school in her university studies. Pre-planning led me to set aside an additional ten dollars a week for that payout. That bill at Ruth Chris was around $650.00 dollars with that child ordering a fat steak that almost covered the entire plate which she ate for the next three days. My husband never offered that incentive again. She also graduated as a valedictorian and had over 60 hours of college credit at the local university as a dual student in high school and college at the same time. This was the compromise to keep her from going to boarding school. There is nothing wrong with boarding school but under no circumstances was I willing to turn any of my children over to anyone else to raise even if that boarding school was offering her a full free ride. As a result, we had her take the ACT exam in the nineth grade and since her score was higher than the state average, we were able to talk the dean of the science department at the university where my husband worked to allow her to be admitted as a special student. One of the resources available to him as a faculty member was his family member qualified for seven hours a semester tuition remission, which meant she could enroll for seven hours, and we had to pay nothing. It required me to pick her up from high school and take her to college daily, so again I would have to make a job change to accommodate that kind of schedule for the next four years. This allowed her to graduate with approximately sixty plus hours of college credit and high school at the same time.

Find the incentive that works for each child as an individual motivation that will help them learn valuable skills and college/career preparation. (5). *Print off the college application for those institutions and identify if that college participates in the uniform college application. Additionally, is there a secondary application in addition to the uniform college application if so, print it off as well.* This was done for the summer following the ninth and tenth grade year.

After the eleventh-grade year all college applications had to be completed before the start of the twelfth-grade year. Once the school portal opens up for submission their application was submitted as most colleges had rolling admissions. During the summertime, your child can work on those and when it is time to apply, they will be familiar with the application and what is needed to complete the application excluding any updates the university has made. A minimum of five hours per week was to be designated for college preparation. College visits were to be completed by the end of the summer after their eleventh-grade school year. We would enhance those college visit with maybe a trip to the local Science Center, zoo or nearby amusement park. I would take all the children on the college tour. The younger of my three were five years apart in age and sometimes that created a challenge but manageable with the bribes of trips to the zoo or parks afterward. They did not have to do it every week, but they did have to reach their summer goals. My children were able to enjoy their senior year as well as prepare for college entry.

Take Away For College Preparation

1. Pull the potential essay questions from those schools as practice essay.
2. Identify what it is going to take to help your child be competitive
3. Identify potential scholarships your child may qualify for at each institution.
4. Give your kids smart gifts and incentives to perform well in school..
5. Print off the college application for those institutions and identify if that college participates in the uniform college application.
6. If there is a secondary application in addition to the uniform college application, print it off as well. This is not an area where you should take short-cuts if you want to help your child build their own wealth.

Religion

Some of you may stop reading at this point, but as evident of how my choice and relationship with my Lord and Savior Jesus Christ has caused my family and our five children to all become successful in their own discipline, even when I had no idea how to help them get to where they wanted to go. My faith has been a steady force in my life that has caused me to do what I needed to do to help our children do in their life resulting in great things. My belief is I can do all things through Christ Jesus who gives me strength. (Philippians 4:13) I have embedded it in my heart and in my mind so when a challenge came up for me or one of my children, we were able to not give up. Having a relationship with my God has given me the strength to endure the late nights and long drives to multiple camps within different direction in the same week. I never took it for granted that driving across the country and safely returning was a guarantee nor a promise. A belief in something stronger or bigger than yourself can be motivation, a strength, and encouragement and a guiding light. My leaning on Philippians 4:13 is what gave me the strength to help them achieve. It is with this scripture I would turn to when things were not clear;

or a lack of directions; there were multiple options, or I was just physically too tried to go any further. Having a relationship with God and God's people in a church became a fundamental basis for other types of support when needed. The church support cannot come from just any church because attending a church is also a method of feeding you and your children's ingredients that will be used to make you and them become who they will be. They must be comfortable there as well as you to allow for the growth that will come. This cannot be a one-sided relationship, meaning you are there to drain out all the resources from the church, but you must also be willing to give as well. That means being involved so that you can be a blessing to others in order to receive your blessings. You may think this will add time to your already busy schedule, and yes it does but God always gave me the strength to continue on. The things we are passionate about we miraculously have the energy to do. Scripture also tells us in Isaiah 40:31 "They who wait for the Lord shall renew their strength; they shall mount up with wings like eagles; they shall run and not be weary; they shall walk and not faint." This scripture contains a great promise of strength for the weary, so when I get tried, I can rely on God to be true to his word and give me strength to go on. This gives me strength to continue to encourage my children to give them the strength when they need it. There will be times when you will need to be the standing post for your kids to lean on. This can be challenging at times because as a parent your child may be hurting, and you hurt because they hurt. This is a prime time when you need God to help you work through, the emotions and be available to help your child. An example of this is when one of my children had a bad breakup with her boyfriend and was trying to complete her graduate studies, and her application for an internship. As a parent, I feel the pain of the emotional breakup and the stress of meeting a deadline to get her application in before the deadline. In this case, I suggested she come home and let's work on what needed to be done to move her to the next phase in her career choice. She did come home, and I listened to what needed to be done and then I talked to her to encourage her to get it done. She was weary but because of my faith and prayer I was confident that God would give me the guidance I needed to help her over that hurdle. We talked through what needed to be done and I challenged her with a series of questions to help her respond to the information needed on the application. I simply told her with God, we will get it done, and we did get it done.

Having a spiritual foundation can cement desires in you and your child that will help them and you to achieve your goals and create additional goals. It can expose you to a controlled environment for which you can safely guard your child's values that will directly impact their goals. It also gave a basis for establishing some direction and goals in life and helping your kids establish goals. My spiritual foundation was a tremendous asset in dealing with having to make sacrifices to accommodate the investment in my children. Emotional feelings can very depend on the day, having to make sacrifices, on behalf of others which I will discuss later in this book.

Unfortunately, we are in a time when society is trying to use religion as a political tool to obtain or maintain power. This is a misconception of religion because it is religion verses relationship. The relationship I have with my Savior has nothing to do with power and everything to do with love. If you are concerned about power, a religious belief is not going to help you help your child become all they are capable of becoming. The search for power requires much energy expenditure which diverts from your investment in yourself or your children. Reaching your goal and helping your children reach their goal will eventually result in a much more valuable power and recognition than any otherwise ascertained fictitious power. At times you and or your child may feel like you are the least among the group; that's ok because scripture tells us that the greatest among you now will be least important then, and those who seem least important now will be the greatest then (paraphrasing Mark 10: 31). The scripture speaks for itself and needs no further explanation.

Now, getting back to helping your children achieve, Proverb 22:6 states, "Train up a child in the way he should go, and when he is old he will not depart from it." This does not mean that they won't run into roadblocks or trouble; it means that the seeds planted inside them will grow. It is a guarantee that you will never plant an orange tree and get apples; it just won't happen. Whatever you instill in your children as they grow up will bear fruit in the future and in their future. You're planting in them seeds such as dedication, endurance, perseverance, honesty, integrity, hard work, and respect, which will bear the greatest fruit in the long term.

Believing you can achieve is like believing in Christ. I never saw him, but I can see the evidence of what his word says and what he has done in my life. I can't see the air I breathe, but I know it's there. As I look out over the ocean and wonder how the water of the ocean stays in place, and the cruise ship, as heavy as it is, stays afloat. I know due to the principle called buoyancy. I haven't seen buoyancy with my own eyes either. Your child may not be able to see themselves as that doctor or earning that Ph.D., behind their name, but they will see the evidence as they work toward that goal and envision small accomplishments each semester. As a parent, you still have to help them see themselves in the position of that doctor, engineer, lawyer, or whatever they choose to become.

Take Away For Religion

The takeaways from religion are.
1. Believe in something that will give you the strength to continue moving you and your children forward. I am always willing to offer Jesus to anyone who wants an undeniable, reliable, and absolute power.
2. Make sure that what you believe in is grounded in truth. Salvation through Jesus Christ is free, because Christ died so it can be free to anyone who is willing to open their heart to him.
3. Have a church home that is supportive and be actively involved in that church. don't just be a recipient of the benefits of that church, but also be a giver to others.
4. There should be some evidence that the God you believe in has done something for you, or that God is real in your life.

Summary of Tools For Success

In order to assist our children in becoming successful, there were some things that we as parents had to instill in them or help them develop for themselves. The first is Will Power or Determination. The second is the ability to work toward the goal without being distracted by short-term wins.

The ability to prolong gratification, resisting short-term temptations of satisfaction in order to meet long-term goals. I trained my children to accept delayed gratification. I taught my children that they have to look toward the long-term goal rather than the short-term achievement. This does not mean there is no recognition for the short-term achievement. There should be some recognition, but keep it in perspective, and always point it toward the long-term goal.

One example of this process is I would use their report cards as a long-term goal. There would be some reward if they were successful in achieving their sought-after goal for their report card at the year-end. At the beginning of the school year, they would set their desired goal for the upcoming school year. This means they had to wait for the entire school year to see if they would be successful. Additionally, during the school year, they would measure their progress and adjust as needed to ensure their success.

I would not allow them to work at a fast-food restaurant (with one exception, which I previously discussed, the McDonalds summer job which was used as a teaching situation.) Preparation for college was their job. That meant working to obtain good grades, a good ACT/SAT score, and other requirements necessary to secure college scholarships. It also included developing the deficiencies they may have that would prevent them from being successful in the pursuit of their long-term goals. It was my belief that some students who work while in high school could be inhibited in performing their best in high school while they are also preparing to meet and make themselves the best candidate for the best and most scholarships. I thought it would be better to sacrifice some of the products students purchase through working part-time at fast food restaurants, such as them tennis shoes or name-brand clothing. Sacrifices were and should be made in other ways, for example, buying the clearance tennis shoes;

they may not be the name of the brand, but your child can wear them just the same. Additionally, this is a teaching opportunity for you to help develop your children. The teaching point for this is to use it to help your child understand that they will have to make sacrifices in order to achieve their goals. Skip the college party to prepare for the exam or just get ahead in the class. Another would be to help them develop a sense of appreciation for themselves. One of my children came home and asked if we would get her some Jordan tennis shoes. I asked her why Jordan's and she responded that all the other kids were wearing them. I then asked her if she knew anything about this person Jordan, and she responded no. My final questions to her were: Why you would want to wear shoes with someone else's name on them that you know nothing about, except they play basketball? What if they are not a nice person? What if they don't believe in what you believe in?, How much were they paying for the shoes if that person was paying for them at all? Teaching them to understand why they would purchase name-brand as compared to investing in their own name. Today, with their own accomplishments they are in a position where they can purchase name-brand now but with more thoughtfulness. This can also teach them to wisely use their money. Additionally, it can be a method of teaching them how to create their own wealth. It is also instilling in them priorities and the process of delayed gratification. This can be the seed you have planted in them that will grow much fruit for the rest of their lives.

The asset of past experiences is motivation to continue moving forward. An example of this is when one of my children was in graduate studies; she became discouraged in her progress and said she didn't believe she could do this. I reminded her of an experience she had when she did a summer program at Davidson College, where she had an opportunity to stay in study an extra week. Upon receiving this honor, she was then informed that there was a requirement that she learn several pieces of music to play at the upcoming concert the following Saturday. She quickly called and said there was no way she could learn all that music in five days. I simply asked her how many notes she could play at a time, and she replied that she could play one. My advice to her was "Well, just learn one note at a time and eventually you will have a stanza learned, and before you know it you will have learned the whole song." I proceeded to tell her I had every confidence in her that she was capable of learning all the pieces and that she would be ready for the concert. She did learn one note at a time and was fully prepared for the concert on that Saturday. This past experience was later used to encourage her in her graduate studies, when she doubted she could do it. I only needed to remind her that she can succeed just as she had with the music program. Therefore, it is important that you use those past experiences in a positive manner to help your child move forward or keep moving forward.

If you serve as the lead character or the person who orchestrates your children's pathway. It is important that you maintain a healthy emotional status. It is important to know when you are emotionally drained and need to replenish yourself. It is also important to know what it takes to replenish yourself. There will be times when you will become frustrated, exhausted, lose determination or focus, will feel like giving up or quitting. In order to be successful and for you to be the lead character, you must be well yourself and keep being emotionally and physically well. This means your emotional intelligence must be on point. You, as the lead character, must determine how to quickly get it back together, as parenting takes no vacation.

It is important that you have some idea of what it takes to maintain your sanity. Additionally, you must also know how to identify when you need to take a break. Also, what does taking a break entail? What is it that can give you immediate relief or rejuvenate you to the point of getting it back together? I am not a psychiatrist or psychologist, and therefore I am not credentialled in offering any diagnosis. My offer is based upon experience and the things that have helped me maintain sanity or a willingness to not give up on my children's future.

The first thing one must do is identify things that can act as a reset button for you. For me, it is as simple as going to the movies. The process of going to the movies is as simple as buying a ticket to the next available movie, popcorn, and a soda. Take notice, I said the next available movie, and this allows me to be able to go anytime and at the same time be conscious of the time I am using. It allows me to not have to plan or orchestrate a trip to the movie, thoughtless, brainless, activity yet highly effective for me. When I was in law school, which was very intense, I used a quick trip to my favorite restaurant to rejuvenate me. This restaurant called Phillips, was located in Baltimore, Maryland. This event took additional planning and savings to make sure it happened. It also served as a reward for finishing the semester. Nothing in either of these required me to exert any significant degree of thoughtfulness. At the time, Southwest had the really cheap flights, less than $100.00 round trip. I had a direct flight that left around 3 pm and arrived in Baltimore in time for dinner at 7:00 P.M. I then checked into the hotel and watched some TV until I fell asleep. There was no setting an alarm clock and no worry about breakfast, there was left over from dinner, or lunch back at Phillips. After lunch, it was time to visit the White Marsh mall for some Christmas shopping or window shopping, but mostly entertaining (free entertainment by people watching) exercise walking through the mall. Nothing during this weekend required me to use any degree of energy, and therefore, did not add any stress. These were simple and relatively inexpensive methods I used to rejuvenate and maintain my sanity and ability to continue to give to others. It also allows my husband to have time alone with our children and for him to assist in caring for them. Since he doesn't cook, I did leave meals prepared and they know how to operate the microwave to warm up their food.

Summary Of Take-A-Ways

EXPECTATIONS

The takeaways are:

1. Make sure there are expectations; it is important that your child knows they are required to have expectations.
2. Start early in your child's life, requiring them to create expectations and make sure the expectations are relative to the child's age.
3. Discuss the expectations with your child and help them understand the needs of each expectation.
4. Require the child to engage in the process, meaning they need to do the research necessary in order to achieve that expectation or goals. In addition to being engaged, the parent must also be supportive and engaged with the child in creating expectations.
5. Parents must also have expectations for themselves. You should not expect your child to do something you are not willing to do. Children are more likely to comply or complete something if they see or know that the parent is willing or has already done the same thing they are being asked to do.

6. Expectations should be thoroughly researched and should always have options or alternatives.
7. Expectations should always have some succeeding expectations. This means that once an expectation is near completion or accomplished, there should be an expectation waiting to be started as the previous one/s ends.

DETERMINATION

Some takeaways are:
1. Use real-life situations as tools to train and/or build confidence, determination, drive, and willpower.
2. Help your child actively work through those situations and preserve the pieces that can be used later in life for either similar or new challenges.
3. Teach your child to see failure not as the enemy, but as an opportunity for greater achievement and growth.

GOAL SETTING

Key takeaways are to:
1. Be realistic
2. Set your own goals as an example
3. Be observant

4. Allow the child to demonstrate their internal passion
5. Conduct the research and include optional outlets if they change their mind
6. Allow the child to set their own goals
7. Debrief or constantly evaluate progress and adjust as needed
8. Talk with your child
9. Listen to your child
10. Provide the support needed for your child to succeed. Support comes in many ways, such as driving them to the various locations needed for them to get the exposure or experience they need.
11. Do not force your goals to be their goals. Let them live their dream, and if you are not living yours, go after your own.
12. Work those plans together. It is a valuable lesson they will need to be successful and survive.

PARENTAL OBSERVATION

Take away from parental observation of each child's capability, identify characteristics, traits, and passions. The greatest benefit is that you get the following:

1. To spend quality beneficial time with your child and develop a lifelong relationship.
2. Knowing your child allows you the ability to help direct them down a certain exploratory path of potential careers.
3. A potential guide to explore options for career choices, summer camps, enrichment programs, and other things that will help your child succeed.
4. Open the opportunity for you to have valuable and productive conversations with your child's teachers and counselors.
5. Cost-saving prevention from wasting money on things such as piano lessons when there is absolutely no interest in the piano.
6. Don't be afraid to make the tough and unpleasant but necessary decisions for the benefit of your child and their future.

7. Be the parent you created and give birth to or adopt that child; it's your responsibility to be the parent.

PARENTING

Takeaways are:

1. Be the parent
2. Make a decision at an early stage, but then transition to what I call exploratory decision making. This is a process where you ask the questions that will help your child make the right decision
3. Know when to identify the lifelong teachable moments that will benefit your child.
4. Always remember each child is an individual and, as such, will be motivated by different things.
5. Do your research to address challenges your child may be face.
6. Allow your child to make the final decision, but make sure they understand the options and consequences of all the options.
7. Never let a teachable moment pass without making the best of it to benefit your child.
8. Don't be afraid to make calculated, tough decisions. They will be painful to all parties involved.

9. Teach your children delayed gratification.
10. Teach your child how to do a SWOT(strengths, weakness, opportunities, threat) analysis when they make any tough decision.

RESOURCES

The takeaways are:

1. Wisely use your resources. Resources, limited or not, should be routed to a specific objective or goal. The resources do not have to be equalized among your children. Having a lot of money is no guarantee that your child will achieve success. The most important factor is to enhance that child's ability to succeed. Additionally, the resources should be directed to improve or promote each child's ability to succeed. For example, math tutoring may be more beneficial for a potential engineering major than dance lessons.
2. Teach your children to utilize and respect the resources available to them. Teaching them to utilize resources effectively will ensure they can make the most of their own resources, and ultimately, you will no longer need to support them, which should be your goal. They should not

have an expectation of living in your basement for life.
3. Teach them to identify the best value for their resources, such as off-season shopping, and carefully research before purchasing.
4. Teach them about the use of credit cards and that they have to be paid back with interest.
5. Help them understand the value of a great credit score.
6. Help them to always have a savings plan, and that rainy days will come, and they will need new tires eventually.

COLLEGE PREPARATION

The takeaways from college preparation are.
1. Pull the potential essay questions from those schools as a practice essay.
2. Identify what it is going to take to help your child be competitive
3. Identify potential scholarships your child may qualify for at each institution.
4. Give your kids smart gifts and incentives to perform well in school.

5. Print off the college application for those institutions or identify if they participate in the uniform college application. Additionally, if there is a secondary application in addition to the uniform college application, print it off as well.

RELIGION

The takeaways from religion are.
1. Believe in something that will give you the strength to continue moving you and your children forward. I am always willing to offer Jesus to anyone who wants an undeniable, reliable, and absolute power.
2. Make sure that what you believe in is grounded in truth. Salvation through Jesus Christ is free, because Christ died so it can be free to anyone who is willing to open their heart to him.
3. Have a church home that is supportive and actively involved in that church. Don't just be a recipient of the benefits of that church, but also be a giver to others.

4. There should be some evidence that the God you believe in has done something for you, or that God is real in your life.

www.ingramcontent.com/pod-product-compliance
Lightning Source LLC
Chambersburg PA
CBHW072149160426
43197CB00012B/2304